FOOTBALL

FOOTBALL: PASS, PUNT, & KICK

BRYANT LLOYD

The Rourke Book Co., Inc.
Vero Beach, Florida 32964

EDITORIAL SERVICES:
Penworthy Learning Systems

Library of Congress Cataloging-in-Publication Data

Lloyd, Bryant. 1942
   Football: pass, punt, and kick / by Bryant Lloyd.
     p. cm. — (Football)
   Includes index
   Summary: Discusses specific elements of football, including the forward pass, punting, and place kicking.
   ISBN 1-55916-210-4 (alk. paper)
   1. Football—Offense—Juvenile literature. [1. Football.]
I. Title II. Series
GV950.7.L54 1997
796.332'2—dc21
                                            97–767
                                              CIP
                                              AC

Printed in the USA

TABLE OF CONTENTS

PASSING

The game is football, but it is not just a game for feet. In most football games, the ball is thrown far more often than it is kicked.

The **forward pass** (FAWR wurd PASS), or throw, is the favorite weapon of many football teams. Many college and professional (NFL) teams throw the ball more often than they run with it. Some high school teams also use the pass as their chief weapon.

The first forward pass was made in a 1906 college game. Passing did not become popular until the 1930's.

Quarterback (black jersey, center) throws a forward pass.

HOW TO THROW A PASS

A football is not perfectly round. Nor is it hand-sized. It is not always easy to throw a football.

To throw, you need a good grip. Place three or four fingers of your throwing hand along the laces of the ball. The laces give the hand a grip.

A coach grips a football properly for throwing.

Looking for a receiver, a quarterback prepares to throw a pass to a teammate.

Cock your arm slightly above the ear on your throwing side. Keep your feet apart about the width of your shoulders. Throw the football in a swift overhand motion, much like a baseball throw.

THE FORWARD PASS

A football can be thrown accurately for a short distance or for more than 60 yards (just over 18 meters)!

A team's passer is its quarterback. The passer throws the ball to a **receiver** (ree SEE ver), the player who catches the ball.

A thrown football spins as it goes through the air. It travels faster and straighter when it is not thrown into the wind.

The forward pass did not become a major part of football offenses until the 1930's.

Quarterback practices passing to teammate before a game.

LATERALS AND PITCH-OUTS

A pass is a forward throw from a player standing behind the **line of scrimmage** (LYN UV SKRIM idj). The line of scrimmage is the point where the ball was put into play.

A player may also pitch the ball sideways or backwards to another player. That is not a pass, but a **pitch-out** (PICH out), when it happens behind the line of scrimmage. Beyond the line of scrimmage or on a kickoff return, a pitch-out is called a **lateral** (LAT er ul). A true forward pass beyond the line of scrimmage or on a kick return is not legal.

In 1970, after the first three Super Bowls, the American Football League and National Football League joined.

With underhand motion, quarterback throws a pitch-out to a running back (out of photo).

CATCHING THE BALL

A good receiver catches the ball with his hands, not his chest or body. After catching the ball, he then brings it to his upper body.

A receiver must watch the flight of the ball closely. Coaches tell receivers to "look the ball into your hands."

Carefully watching the ball, a receiver makes the catch with his hands.

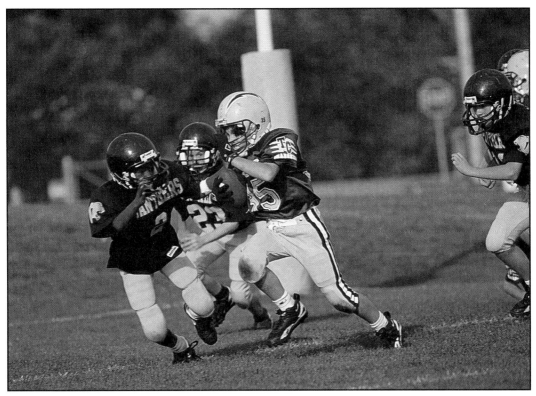

A good receiver catches the ball before trying to run with it.

Coaches also tell players to catch the ball before looking away or trying to run with it.

Receivers who look away at the last instant often drop the pass.

PUNTING

The punt is a kick usually used on fourth down. The punt turns the football over to a team's opponent.

A punt begins with the football being **snapped** (SNAPT), or hiked, from the team's center to its punter. The punter catches the ball and kicks as he drops it toward his kicking foot.

A good punt travels high as well as far, which gives the kicking team time to rush down the field and surround the punt receiver.

Canadian football fields are longer and wider than fields in the U.S. Canadians play with 12-man teams and have three downs instead of four.

Punter steps into kicking motion. Punter will release the ball a split second before kicking it.

CATCHING A PUNT

Catching a punt requires skill and nerve. A punt receiver must decide quickly whether to catch the football or let it bounce.

If he catches the ball, he can run with it. Tacklers, though, can swarm over him as soon as he touches the ball and perhaps jar it loose.

The punt receiver can also decide to signal with his hand for a fair catch. After a fair catch, he cannot run. He cannot be tackled either.

Catching a punted football requires the receiver to train his eyes on the flight of the ball.

PLACE KICKING

A place kick is a kick of the football from a certain place on the field. Place kicks occur on kickoffs, extra points, and field goal attempts.

For a place kick, the football is usually held upright. It leans toward the kicker with laces facing away.

Kicker races toward a football held upright by a kicking tee.

*Head down, keeping his eyes on the ball, a place kicker boots
the football.*

The football is usually held by a kicking tee for
kickoffs. A player other than the kicker holds the
ball upright for extra point and field goal
attempts. He is called the **holder** (HOL der). He
must work quickly to place the ball in position.

KICKING TRUE

Kicking accuracy is important. A kickoff, for example, must stay in the field. If not, the receiving team gains extra yards from a **penalty** (PEN ul tee) against the kicker.

An extra point or field goal kick must go over the crossbar and between the goal posts.

The defensive team can block a kicking attempt.

The only professional team in recent history to finish a season without a loss was the Miami Dolphins. Miami finished the 1973 season 17-0.

Perfect placement of the ball in the tee and good kicking form help a place kicker stay on target.

GLOSSARY

forward pass (FAWR wurd PASS) — a ball thrown forward from behind the line of scrimmage

holder (HOL der) — the player who holds the football for another player to kick

lateral (LAT er ul) — a throw of the football to a player who is beside or behind the thrower when the thrower is beyond the line of scrimmage

line of scrimmage (LYN UV SKRIM idj) — an imaginary line across a football field; place where the ball is put after a play

penalty (PEN ul tee) — a loss of yards or downs for breaking a rule of the game

pitch-out (PICH out) — a sideways or backwards toss of the football from one player to another behind the line of scrimmage

receiver (ree SEE ver) — any player who catches a forward pass; one who sets up in a football formation as if he might catch a pass

snap (SNAP) — the movement of the football by the center to another player

With a receiver in his sights, a quarterback cocks his arm to throw.

23

INDEX